Design Your Own Quilts
Judy Hopkins

ONE-OF-A-KIND QUILTS: REVISED AND UPDATED WITH 55 NEW QUILTS

That Patchwork Place®

An Imprint of Martingale & Company

DEDICATION

For Jeanie Smith, who is both wise and amusing.

ACKNOWLEDGMENTS

Special thanks are extended to:

The One-of-a-Kind quilters: those who've been asking for the book, those who submitted quilts for consideration, and those whose quilts are included; without you, there would be nothing;

Peggy Hinchey, Julie Kimberlin, and Kathy Mosher, for their fine hand and machine quilting;

Diane Nielsen, for "Little Liberty";

Marsha McCloskey and Fabric Sales Corporation, for providing fabrics from the Staples line for several of the quilts.

CREDITS

Editor-in-Chief .... Kerry I. Smith
Technical Editor .... Melissa A. Lowe
Managing Editor .... Judy Petry
Design Director .... Cheryl Stevenson
Text Designer .... Kay Green
Cover Designer .... Trina Stahl
Copy Editor .... Liz McGehee
Proofreader .... Leslie Phillips
Illustrator .... Laurel Strand
Photographer .... Brent Kane
Production Assistant .... Marijane E. Figg

Design Your Own Quilts
© 1998 by Judy Hopkins

Martingale & Company
PO Box 118
Bothell, WA 98041-0118 USA

Printed in Canada
03 02 01 00 99 98   6 5 4 3 2 1

Library of Congress Cataloging-in-Publication Data

Hopkins, Judy,
    Design your own quilts / Judy Hopkins.
        p. cm.
    "That Patchwork Place."
    "Revised and updated with 55 new quilts."
    Includes bibliographical references.
    ISBN 1-56477-210-1
    1. Quilting—Patterns. 2. Patchwork—Patterns.
3. Wall hangings.
I. Title.
TT835.H5696 1998
746.46—dc21   97-41263
                                          CIP

Contents

Preface

Welcome to the twenty-first-century version of my 1989 book, *One-of-a-Kind Quilts!* The original book, out of print for a number of years, was something of a cult classic, discovered and embraced by little pockets of quilters everywhere. More than a quarter of the 107 quilt entries in That Patchwork Place's fifteenth anniversary quilt contest (1991) were One-of-a-Kind quilts—including the grand-prize winner, made by Pat Maixner Magaret, who later co-authored the immensely successful That Patchwork Place book *Watercolor Quilts.*

In the summer of 1990, during the height of tourist season, the Anchorage Museum of History and Art exhibited the quilts from the original *One-of-a-Kind Quilts.* It was sort of a "local-quilters-make-good" celebration—all of the quilts in the book were made by friends and colleagues from Anchorage and its neighboring communities. Once in a while, one of us would spend a little spare time at the museum, following the visitors around and shamelessly eavesdropping on their comments about the quilts. One day, an increasingly agitated woman made her way through the gallery. When she reached the last quilt, she turned to her companion and announced: "These people have copied every single quilt in that book I bought a couple of months ago!" She had no idea she was looking at the originals.

I've had a lot of fun with One-of-a-Kind quilts for a lot of years—making them, teaching other quilters how to make them, and listening to people talk about them. I've been absolutely awestruck by the unique pieces that quilters using this approach have created and shared. Naturally, I was delighted when That Patchwork Place gave me the opportunity to refresh the One-of-a-Kind

design concept for another generation of quilters. The old words have been polished up, and a few new ones have been added. The quilts are all new, made by talented and inventive One-of-a-Kind quilters from across the United States and Canada. There's something here to inspire everyone, from simple and scrappy quilts that are meant to be loved and used to gorgeous pieces that would be at home in any gallery. I think they're all quite wonderful.

So, for all of you who have been asking—here we go, again. And to those who have just discovered these simple blueprints for creative quilts, come on along—you're in for a treat!

4

Introduction

Some days, I just want to turn off my head and make a nice little everyday quilt. I may be tired of working on the intricate, interminable piece for the major exhibit and need to unwind with something less demanding. Perhaps I am in the mood to attack the overflowing scrap box or make a quick but special thank-you for a friend— but I don't want to draft patterns, struggle with new techniques, or run to the shop in search of a particular shade of blue. I want to work effortlessly, using the materials at hand and techniques I already know well; I want to enjoy the process and have some confidence I will be satisfied with the result.

The lighthearted everyday quilt should be a part of every quiltmaker's repertoire. Though we are no longer required by necessity to produce utility quilts, there is still a place for the classic utility-quilt approach, which downplays planning and encourages original solutions: Use it up! Make it do! These winsome quilts, quickly patched together from bits and pieces and spare parts, are always interesting, often amusing, and invariably unique.

But everyday quilts require an offhand, relaxed approach that can be a problem for those of us who crave direction, systems, and order. I had difficulty capturing their unstudied liveliness in my work until I devised a working method that provided both structure and opportunities for creative decision making and resulted in quilts that were truly one of a kind.

One-of-a-Kind quilts are structured scrap quilts—everyday quilts that feature a planned theme or focal area surrounded by blocks made in a variety of patterns, with the overall design developing as the piece is made. Every quilt is different; the quilts presented in these pages are vivid testament to that fact. Some are nice little everyday quilts, pleasant and uncomplicated. Some are positively stunning. Others are decidedly offbeat. All of them are successful designs— and all were made using the simple step-by-step process I share with you in this book.

The historic antecedents of One-of-a-Kind quilts are traced in "Roots" (page 6)—the framed-center quilts of the British Isles and the American utility quilt. "An Overview" (pages 7–11) explains the key ingredients of the One-of-a-Kind technique: the progressive select-make-audition working method that promotes organized originality, the twelve basic blueprints and their variations, and the menu of block patterns.

"Making the One-of-a-Kind Quilt" (pages 12–26) takes you step by step through the theme blocks and the background blocks, covering everything from cutting and construction techniques to the creative decisions that are made along the way. Suggestions for completing the quilts are included. An "idea" section (pages 56–65) suggests projects and variations on the basic approach.

Read through the text to get an overall view of the process. Don't worry about absorbing the details; things will fall into place as you make your first One-of-a-Kind quilt. Browse through "A Gallery of Creative Quilts" (pages 66–88) for ideas and inspiration. Then turn to "The Method" section on page 7 and get started.

The process is easy. The quilts are simple, fast, and fun to make—they've been known to take over and design themselves. I've provided a flexible framework on which you can build quilts that are uniquely your own. Enjoy!

Roots

The roots of the One-of-a-Kind quilt lie in the early framed-center quilts of the British Isles. These charming and highly original pieces might aptly be called "utility medallions."

The framed-center format was a popular method of setting out a nineteenth-century British bedcover. The quilts often featured fine embroidery, appliqué work, or decorative printed panels as elaborate central motifs; cotton manufacturers of the day designed and printed panels especially for use in these quilts.

The central panel was surrounded by a series of borders (frames), usually all different, providing "great opportunity for a variety of different patterns in one piece of work."[1] The frames, usually made from simple combinations of squares, triangles, and rectangles, often were quite casual in comparison with the formal central blocks. In her discussion of framed-center quilts in *A Practical Guide to Patchwork from the Victoria and Albert Museum*, Linda Parry notes that "the composition of the quilt is likely to have been developed during construction rather than been designed in advance."[2]

We can speculate, then, that these quiltmakers planned distinctive blocks or purchased special fabrics for the central motifs and used what was on hand for the "frames," constructing the borders in what Averil Colby calls "the natural and spontaneous spirit which is so essentially part of patchwork."[3] Janet Rae, writing for the British Quilt Heritage Project in *Quilt Treasures of Great Britain*, suggests that the frames were pieced in strips, a thrifty and easy way of working: "You could, after all, sit with (and easily transport) a small workbasket and make limitless numbers of patchwork strips—against the day when you had enough strips to put together a whole quilt. Certainly this would have explained the disregard for the positioning of light and dark colours and a general lack of planning so evident in some of the more simple frame quilts.... There were obvious difficulties in working out measurements, especially when it came to the corners."[4]

In *Traditional British Quilts*, Dorothy Osler commends the framed-center style to contemporary readers: "As a patchwork design it has many attractions for the potential quiltmaker. It provides the basic framework for making either simple or complex designs and for adapting and experimenting with different patchwork patterns within the border areas and the medallion centre itself."[5]

The framed-center quilt has much in common with the penny-wise American utility quilt and the pleasant chaos of the child's learning piece. Made from leftover blocks and scrap-bag accumulations, these unpretentious quilts often feature a focal point surrounded by blocks made up in a variety of patterns. Though the overall composition may be quite formal, the approach to the individual elements is decidedly carefree. Pieces are placed where they fit or are made to fit with unceremonious chopping or by adding strips or checkerboards. Corners may not meet; rows may not line up. These are everyday quilts, inspired by necessity. Their makers imposed order as best they could, within the limits of time and materials, and produced unique pieces that have been called "examples of unlearned artistry."[6]

The One-of-a-Kind Quilt: An Overview

One-of-a-Kind quilts are the contemporary counterparts of these early British and American examples. Like their predecessors, they reflect a disciplined spontaneity. They have a planned theme, surrounded by blocks made from a variety of patterns and fabrics. Planning is "as you go," with each decision guided by the work that has gone before.

In the contemporary interpretation, however, overall organization is more flexible. The theme might not be confined to a single central block; the background blocks may or may not be organized into formal, medallionlike borders. Choices you make will determine the character of the quilt: casual, elegant, or somewhere in between. An original result is virtually guaranteed; two quiltmakers working from the same set of basic rules will produce two entirely different quilts.

The process is simple and straightforward. You start with a blueprint (one of the twelve provided on pages 32–55) and a theme—a planned focal point. The theme is surrounded by an assortment of 4" x 4" background blocks, which you choose from a menu in several select-make-audition steps.

Let's begin by taking a quick look at the key ingredients: the step-by-step method, the blueprints, and the menu. The steps, from choosing a blueprint to finishing the quilt, are thoroughly discussed in "Making the One-of-a-Kind Quilt," starting on page 12.

The Method: Step by Step through the One-of-a-Kind Quilt

- Select a blueprint.
- Decide on a theme or topic (the focal point).
- Make the theme block(s).
- Assemble fabrics that support your theme.
- Make the background blocks, one step at a time. (The number of steps will vary, depending on the blueprint you've selected.)

    Step 1: Select and make a set of background blocks from Row 1 of the menu. Audition the background blocks with the theme block(s) on a design wall.

    Step 2: Select, make, and audition a set of background blocks from Row 2 of the menu.

    Step 3: Select, make, and audition a second set of blocks from Row 1.

    Step 4: Select, make, and audition a second set of blocks from Row 2.

    Step 5: Select and make filler blocks.

- Frame or border the theme block(s) if needed.
- Set the blocks together, add borders, and complete the quilt.

THE BLUEPRINTS

Blueprints for quilts in twelve different sizes start on page 32. A quick reference chart is included on pages 30–31. These plans provide the basic framework for One-of-a-Kind quilts; they define the theme area and set out the steps for the surrounding background blocks. Look at Blueprint 4 below.

Blueprint 4

7 x 9 grid
28" x 36" without borders
Theme area: 16 squares

47 background blocks:
Step 1: 22 from Row 1
Step 2: 12 from Row 2
Step 3: 8 from Row 1
Step 4: 5 fillers

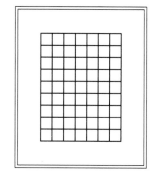

All of the plans are based on 4" x 4" grids. The layouts range from 4 x 5 (four blocks across and five down) in Blueprint 1, to 10 x 10 (ten blocks across and ten down) in Blueprint 12. Since each square of the grid represents a 4" (finished) block, the Blueprint 1 quilt (4 x 5 grid) measures 16" x 20" without borders; the Blueprint 12 quilt (10 x 10 grid) measures 40" x 40". Any of the rectangular plans can be rotated 90° for a horizontal format.

The theme occupies about 25% of the quilt's surface; the larger the quilt, the more grid squares are devoted to the theme. This focal point can be organized in blocks or in other configurations; each plan includes several options for structuring the theme area.

The number of background blocks and the steps for completing them vary from blueprint to blueprint, again depending on the size of the quilt. For the smaller quilts, the 4" blocks are completed in three or four steps; for the larger quilts, in five steps. The number of background blocks to be made at each step is indicated on each blueprint.

One of two things will determine the plan you choose to work with: the size of the quilt you wish to make or the theme you've decided to use. If you want to make a quilt of a certain size, make or use theme blocks that fit that plan. If you have blocks available to use as the theme or have a particular theme in mind, choose a plan that accommodates the theme.

THE MENU

"The Menu" is a collection of patterns for background blocks. The twenty different patterns are separated into two groups: Row 1 and Row 2. The ten blocks with four or fewer pieces comprise Row 1; those with five or more pieces are grouped in Row 2. Blocks selected from Row 1 will occupy about 50% of the quilt's surface; the busier Row 2 blocks take up about 25%.

The numbers under the block outlines on the menu (1.1, 2.1, etc.) identify the individual blocks and their rows. The number-plus-letter designations (1A, 8K, etc.) indicate which quick-cut shapes or templates are used to make that particular block and the number of pieces to cut. Block 2.8, for example, requires four of shape K (2⅞" x 2⅞" squares, cut once diagonally) and one piece cut from Template N.

Cutting dimensions for the quick-cut shapes are given at right. Basic templates for the other shapes are provided on page 10. Note that there are no I and O shapes. Stitching tips for a couple of the trickier blocks appear on page 11.

Row 1	Row 2
1.1: 1A	2.1: 2G, 4K
1.2: 2B	2.2: 9L
1.3: 3C	2.3: 16M
1.4: 4D	2.4: 2E, 8M

Row 1 *continued*	**Row 2** *continued*
1.5: 4E	2.5: 8K
1.6: 2F	2.6: 8K
1.7: 1F, 2G	2.7: 8K
1.8: 4G	2.8: 4K, 1N
1.9: 2H, 1J	2.9: 4K, 4P
1.10: 4H	2.10: 1F, 4K

QUICK CUTTING THE SHAPES

A—4½" square

B—2½" x 4½" rectangle

C—Use template.

D—1½" x 4½" rectangle

E—2½" square

F—Divided 4⅞" square yields 2.

G—Twice-divided 5¼" square yields 4.

H—Use template.

J—Use template.

K—Divided 2⅞" square yields 2.

L—Use template.

M—1½" square

N—Use template.

P—Use template.

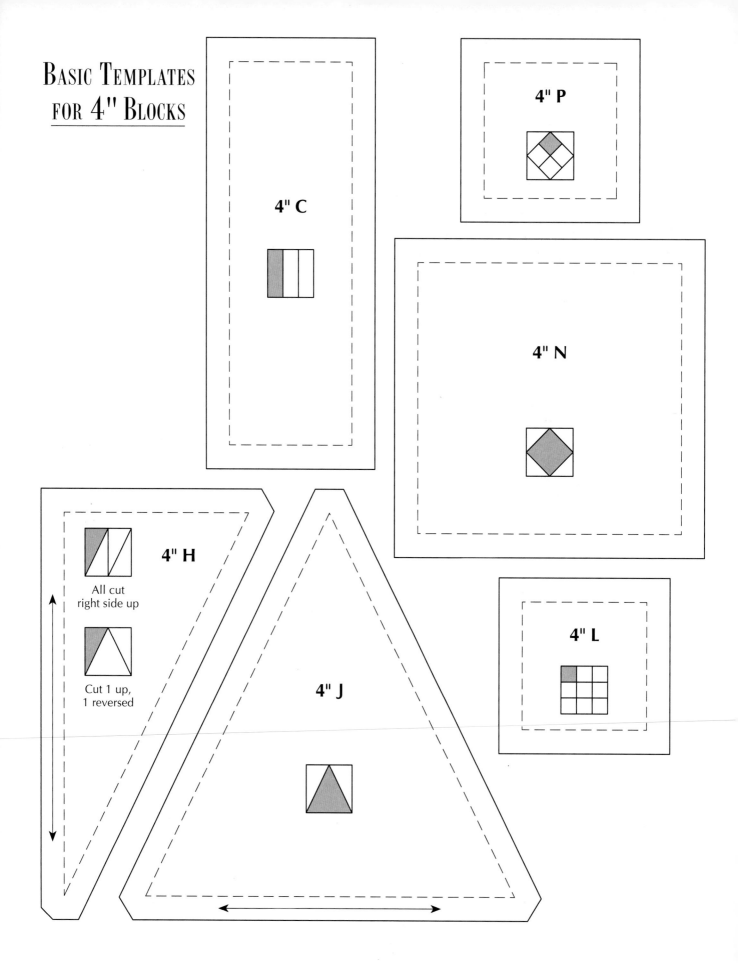

BASIC TEMPLATES
FOR 4" BLOCKS

4" C

4" P

4" N

4" H

All cut
right side up

Cut 1 up,
1 reversed

4" J

4" L

STITCHING TIPS

Flying Geese Units (Block 2.1)

1. Join the left-hand triangle. Match points (A) and bottom edges; sew in the direction of the arrow. Press seam toward the smaller triangle.

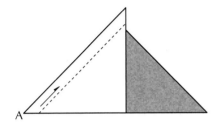

2. Join the right-hand triangle. Start at the arrow. Your ¼" seam should exactly intersect the 90° angle where the two smaller triangles meet, as shown in the magnified portion of the drawing. Adjust the position of the loose triangle until the seam lines up correctly. Take a few stitches, then match points (B) and finish stitching the seam. Press seam toward the smaller triangle.

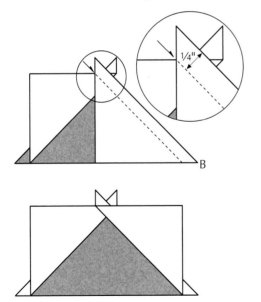

Square-in-a-Square Units (Blocks 2.8 and 2.9)

1. Join the opposing triangles first, centering the triangles on the square. The triangle points will extend about ⅜" beyond the edges of the square. Press seams toward the triangles.

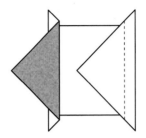
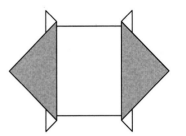

2. Join the remaining triangles. Your ¼" seam should exactly intersect the 90° angle where the two triangles meet at both the top and bottom ends of the seam, as shown in the magnified areas of the drawing. Adjust the position of the loose triangle until the seam lines up correctly at A. Take a few stitches, then adjust the points at B and finish stitching the seam. Press seams toward the triangles.

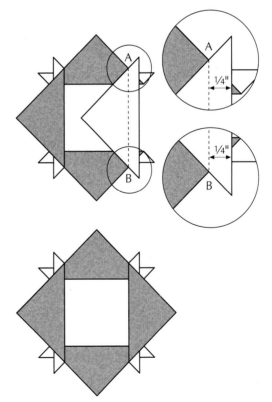

Making the One-of-a-Kind Quilt

In "The Method" (page 7), I tidily listed the steps for making a One-of-a-Kind quilt. In the real world, of course, things are not so tidy. We get into a kind of chicken-and-egg situation with the first few steps (select a blueprint, decide on a theme or topic, make theme blocks). Things don't always proceed in the order given! Often, you start a One-of-a-Kind quilt because you have something on hand that you want to use as a theme: leftovers from a previous project, a printed panel, or a commemorative T-shirt. When you're working this way, the "make-the-theme-block" step is moot. You already have a theme; the number, size, and shape of the existing theme block(s) will point you toward a particular plan.

The information in this chapter, then, may not be presented in the order in which you'll use it. I'd suggest a quick read-through, so you'll get a sense of what's discussed, and where. We'll start by talking about the theme area of the quilt, move on to a brief and general discussion on color and fabric, then examine the background blocks, from cutting and construction through the select-make-audition steps. Later, we'll talk about finishing techniques, then walk though the decision-making process that produced "White Hemstitch," a medallion-style One-of-a-Kind quilt with a pieced, traditional theme.

USEFUL TOOLS

Rotary cutting and design-wall composition are important elements of the One-of-a-Kind technique. A few specialized tools are helpful in the cutting and composition process; you might want to consider a few of my favorites.

There are several different sizes and brands of rotary cutters. I find the 1⅛"-diameter rotary cutter more manageable than the 1¾"-diameter size. An added advantage is that blades for the small cutter cost less than blades for the larger size, so one isn't so slow to replace a dull blade. For efficient quick cutting, you'll need an assortment of cutting rulers with ⅛" markings. My favorite is the 8" Bias Square®, available from That Patchwork Place. Although the Bias Square was developed for a specialized purpose, it's an excellent general-purpose cutting guide; the markings and measurements are very easy to read, reducing the chances for error. When cutting small pieces like those that make up the background blocks, I use a cutting mat that's about 12" square; this convenient size is currently obtainable only if you cut down a larger mat.

A piece of needlepunch or Pellon fleece pinned to a foam-core panel makes a good design wall. When you smooth your blocks onto the fleece, it "grips" the blocks so you can audition and easily rearrange them as desired. The blocks will generally stay in place without pinning, though it is wise to stop and pin occasionally. Carefully composed quilts have been known to fall off design walls into nondescript heaps!

Another design-wall option is a large piece of gray felt. On mine, I've drawn a 12 x 12 grid of 4½" squares (the raw-edge-to-raw-edge measurement of the background blocks). The grid simplifies composition; if I'm making a Blueprint 7 quilt, which is based on an 8 x 10 grid, I simply outline an 8 x 10 working area on the felt grid with pieces of twill tape. However, felt has less grip than fleece, so blocks must be pinned when placed, and unpinned and re-pinned when moved.

A reducing glass is a wonderful aid in the composition process. It is the opposite of a magnifying glass; it makes images smaller instead of larger. Problem areas seem to leap out at you when your perspective is altered. You can get the same effect by looking through the wrong end of a pair of binoculars or through the viewfinder of a camera; you can also alter your perspective by taking off your glasses, by looking at your quilt's reflection in a mirror, or by turning your design wall sideways or upside down. It's handier to have a reducing glass. They're available at many art-, office-, or drafting-supply stores; perhaps your quilt shop carries them. They're expensive, but worth it—a good item for your Christmas list!

Another optional-but-valuable item for the serious quiltmaker is an inexpensive Polaroid camera. With an instant picture, you can "save" a composition you like and continue to experiment with other arrangements. A photo of your final design will help you sort out which side is up and what goes where if your blocks get scrambled on their trip from the design wall to the sewing machine.

THE THEME BLOCKS

The theme area is the focal point of the quilt—a surface to express a mood or idea, display a pieced or appliquéd block, or showcase a special piece of fabric or other handiwork. Usually, the theme area is organized into blocks based on 4" multiples; several options are available for each plan. In Blueprint 4, for instance, the theme occupies sixteen squares of the 7 x 9 grid. This can be accomplished in several ways: by using four 8" theme blocks (Blueprint 4A), four 4" and three 8" theme blocks (Blueprint 4B), or a single 16" theme block (Blueprint 4C). All theme-block sizes given are finished sizes; be sure to allow for seams.

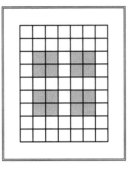

Blueprint 4A
Four 8" theme blocks

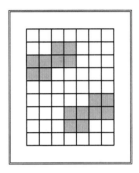

Blueprint 4A variation

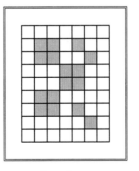

Blueprint 4B
Four 4" and three 8" theme blocks

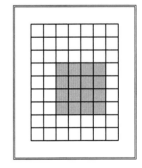

Blueprint 4C
One 16" theme block

The theme blocks can be placed anywhere within the grid; the shaded areas on the blueprints are merely ideas. Both "Stars and Bars" (page 53) and "Televangelists" (page 74) were made from Blueprint 11, using three 12" theme blocks. In "Stars and Bars," the theme blocks are grouped to form a horizontal bar that runs from one edge of the quilt to the other; in "Televangelists," the theme blocks are scattered across the quilt's surface. You might start with the theme blocks in one position and change your mind as you go along.

The possibilities for themes are unlimited. If you've examined the quilts in this book, you may already have several theme motifs in mind. Themes can be representational; consider patchwork pictures of fish, houses, trees, butterflies, or boats. Traditional pieced or appliquéd blocks are another possibility. How about Card Trick, Ohio Star, Night and Noon, Lancaster Rose, or Sunbonnet Sue?

You can use your theme area to showcase printed panels, embroidered blocks, silk-screened images, an especially wonderful fabric, exquisite quilting in white-on-white, stenciled motifs, or cyanotypes. Consider hand-painted, marbled, or airbrushed textiles; ethnic prints; or fabrics that have been textured by folding, crushing, pleating, or weaving. Search your shelves for that linen handkerchief embroidered by your grandmother, the strip-pieced landscape started in a workshop, or the single Dresden Plate block uncovered at a garage sale.

Fresh Start or Spare Parts?

Your theme blocks might be planned and made specifically for the quilt (the fresh start), or you might take a spare-parts approach, using leftovers or rejects from other projects. In either case, the theme—the new idea or the spare parts on hand—may dictate which blueprint or which variation you decide to use. Some of the blueprints require a single theme block; others use two or more. In some plans, all of the theme blocks are the same size; others call for blocks of different sizes.

If you want to make a hens-and-chicks quilt, a blueprint that includes both 4" and 8" theme blocks would be a logical choice. Maybe you have two similar or identical "orphan" blocks stuck away in a drawer somewhere; try a blueprint that calls for two blocks of the same size. If you want a quilt that's not dominated by a single, large theme block, select a blueprint that calls for several smaller blocks. Repeat a single pattern or create different blocks on the same subject: a gingham dog and a calico cat, a Bachelor's Puzzle and an Old Maid's Ramble, an appliquéd bear and pieced Bear Tracks.

Grandmother's Choice

Grandmother's Favorite

Dutchman's Puzzle

Yankee Puzzle

Road to Heaven

Steps to the Altar

Cutting and piecing instructions can be found in *Around the Block with Judy Hopkins* (That Patchwork Place).

Sizing Things Up

There is a natural tendency for One-of-a-Kind quilters to work at getting their theme blocks to the "proper" size as soon as they've decided which blueprint to use. Wait! *Read this section before you start chopping off or adding on.*

If you're using a focus fabric, a silk-screen print or some other kind of whole cloth, or an oversized pieced or appliquéd block for a theme, don't cut it down just yet. For now, just fold in the edges until your theme piece is the size your blueprint calls for. You may find later that your theme wants to be a larger size or a different shape.

Undersized blocks and rectangular, circular, or other irregularly shaped forms will eventually need to be built up, to make the theme block fit the space. Obviously, if your theme is a traditional block that must be set on point, some kind of frame will be required (see "Setting Theme Blocks on Point" on page 16). Don't frame now! We'll talk about framing options here, to give you some things to think about, but don't decide about the style of the frame or the fabrics and colors until you've made and placed the background blocks. A frame that seems appropriate early in the process may not work as well when all the elements are combined.

Sometimes framing is a deliberate design choice. In a busy, high-contrast quilt, you may want to isolate the theme block from the background, either by framing or by allowing enough margin between the motif and the edge of the block to provide visual separation. If you're making a theme block specifically for the quilt and know you'll want to set it apart with borders, you'll have to make the block smaller than the size called for to allow for the frame.

You might frame the theme block with a simple border made from a single strip of fabric, or use several rows of strips or wedges in different widths and colors. You could mat the theme block like a picture, in an oval or round frame. The empty corners left by on-point theme blocks could be filled with full or partial background blocks.

The framing can be either emphasized or downplayed. Framing that holds its own against other elements may be the best choice for some quilts. In others, you might want to use low-impact framing, where matching fabrics, colors, or values fill the space without distinctly separating the theme from the background.

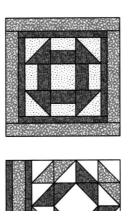
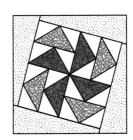

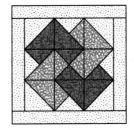
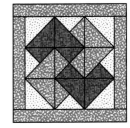

Blending   Contrasting

Setting Theme Blocks on Point

If you're working with spare parts, you need to be aware that if you turn a standard-size theme (like an 8" or 12" block or cut of fabric) on point and fill the corners with triangles, the resulting unit is not going to fit the 4" grid. A 12" (finished) block set on point will finish to a 17" square. To make this fit your grid, you would need to build it up to fill a 20" square. An 8" (finished) block, set on point, finishes to an 11⅓" square and would have to be built up to fill a 12" square.

When you're starting fresh, you can make the theme blocks in a size that, when turned on point, will fit the grid. An 8½" (finished) theme block on point fills a 12" (finished) square. For corners, cut two 6⅞" squares and divide them once diagonally. Follow the stitching tips for square-in-a-square units on page 11.

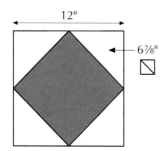

12"

← 6⅞"

Theme block 8½"
(finished size)

An 11¼" (finished) theme block on point fills a 16" (finished) square. Fill the corners with shapes A and F as shown; for plain corners, cut two 8⅞" squares and divide them once diagonally.

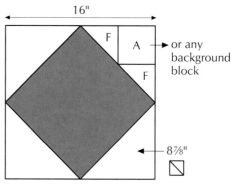

16"

F A → or any background block

F

← 8⅞"

Theme block 11¼"
(finished size)

A 14⅛" (finished) theme block on point fills a 20" (finished) square. For corners, cut two 10⅞" squares and divide them once diagonally.

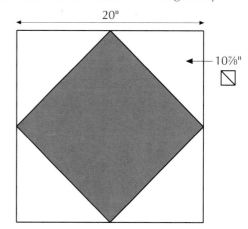

20"

← 10⅞"

Theme block 14⅛"
(finished size)

Variations on the Theme

The theme does not have to be confined to square, precisely sized blocks—it simply needs to occupy about 25% of the quilt's surface. The number of squares that should be devoted to the theme is indicated on each blueprint.

You can use any shape that will fit the 4" grid. For example, the theme can be arranged in rectangles, such as 8" x 12" or 12" x 16"; stretched into 4"-wide strips; bent into L shapes; or arranged in irregular shapes. A strong, dominant fabric can draw the eye and provide a focus even when fractured into 4" squares and distributed across the surface of the quilt. Any configuration will do, as long as the theme area is covered. Several of the quilt plans include grids shaded to suggest some possibilities. The sixteen-square theme area of the Blueprint 4 quilt, for instance, can be covered in a number of ways:

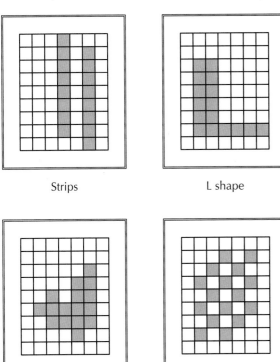

Strips   L shape

Irregular shape   Fractured

Be flexible. If your plan calls for a twenty-square theme area and your theme refuses to cover more than eighteen squares or insists on covering twenty-two, bend the rule to fit the quilt. Oversized orphan blocks may have to appropriate space that would otherwise be filled with background blocks. Spaces around undersized theme blocks can be filled with whole or partial background blocks, or with frames.

Whether you use blocks or organize your theme area into other shapes, remember that the theme can be placed anywhere within the grid. You can center your theme block(s) by moving them 2" in any direction; fill the resulting gaps with partial background blocks. You can even let your theme block(s) extend outside of the grid into the borders of the quilt. Tinker with placement during the audition phase until the look of the quilt suits you.

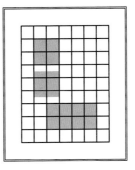
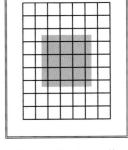

Centered vertically   Centered horizontally
                              and vertically

Occasionally, a quilt will reject its theme block; the background and the theme begin to look as if they belong to two different quilts. If things feel wrong, try replacing the theme block. Maybe the right theme is an interesting piece of fabric that's been on your shelf all along.

Choosing Fabrics to Support Your Theme

Once you've made (or found!) your theme block(s), buy or pull a range of fabrics that go with your theme and that fit the look you want to achieve. For a pine-tree theme, you would probably want to work with an assortment of greens; a winter theme might be executed in whites, grays, and icy blues. If you're using a preprinted panel, a piece of embroidery, a cut of a favorite fabric, or an orphan block as the theme, select coordinating colors and fabrics for the background blocks.

You may be trying for a particular style or mood. Soft florals feel sweet or romantic; jazzy geometrics look modern or upbeat; plaids and stripes say "folk" or "country." An autumn mood calls for reds, oranges, rusts, and browns; a spring mood wants yellows, lavenders, pinks, soft blues, and greens. Scrappy quilts sport an abundance of colors and values; sophisticated quilts are often more controlled. Quilts from other eras feature distinctive colors and prints that you can adopt for a period look.

You'll see that some of the quilts pictured in this book are multifabric quilts, others use only three or four different fabrics. "Blueprints" (page 35) uses just one! Some of the quilts were made entirely from collected or scrap fabrics; others were made from fabrics purchased specifically for the quilt.

I often start with eight fabrics. Sometimes I use them all and add more; sometimes I end up using just two or three. Carol Solt, a veteran One-of-a-Kind teacher, suggests you cut a 4½" square of each of the fabrics you're considering; place these on your design wall along with your theme block(s) and see which fabrics "talk to you" or "talk together."

Here are a few general tips on color and fabric selection that work for me:

- Resist overmatching; variation adds interest.

- Include an accent. This is often a temperature contrast, like a warm red to spark up an assortment of cool blues.

- Give intense colors support in the form of a shadow or echo. Using a bit of tan or peach can make a bright orange acceptable.

- Consider adding a color surprise. Occasionally substitute a navy for a brown, a pink for a rust.

Neutrals (white, black, gray, brown, beige, tan, ivory, taupe) and the natural colors of wood, stone, earth, sky, and metal (umber, ochre, earth red, olive drab, forest green, gray blue, indigo) are the quilt colorist's secret weapons. Neutrals can be added to any color scheme without changing it. Naturals add interest without drawing attention to themselves. The dirty-gold color that quiltmakers have found so useful is a natural; so is khaki, a favorite of the more adventurous designers. Neutrals and naturals can help weld other colors together; they slip into the background or neutralize colors that resist being combined.

If you're using prints, select with an eye to visual texture. Include large-scale prints, small-scale prints, florals, and geometrics. Plan to carry one or two fabrics or colors throughout the quilt; repetition will unify the surface.

You may want to beef up your fabric collection with some unusual fabrics. Look for things you don't ordinarily buy, like plaids, checks, stripes, polka dots, large florals, ethnic prints, or pictorial (conversational) prints. A ¼-yard or ½-yard cut is plenty; I rarely buy more than ½ yard of any fabric. If you limit your purchases to small cuts, you can build a fabric collection that is rich in variety and both stimulating and challenging in its potential.

THE BACKGROUND BLOCKS

The area of the quilt not occupied by the theme is filled with 4" background blocks, which you select from the menu of block patterns. The process is divided into several distinct steps. At each step, you select and make a certain number of blocks from the menu, auditioning those blocks with the theme blocks on the design wall before proceeding to the next select-make-audition step. The number of steps—and the number of blocks to make at each step—varies with each plan. In Blueprint 4, for example, the 4" background blocks are completed in four steps:

- 🖐 *Step 1:* 22 from Row 1
- 🖐 *Step 2:* 12 from Row 2
- 🖐 *Step 3:* 8 from Row 1
- 🖐 *Step 4:* 5 fillers

This step-wise approach eliminates the need for extensive preplanning, lets you focus on one small set of decisions at a time, and allows the design to evolve as construction proceeds. Decisions you've made at one step will influence the decisions that follow. Sometimes, after the first few steps have been completed, subsequent choices will seem almost inevitable; in effect, the quilt takes over and designs itself.

Some quiltmakers have difficulty with this intuitive, plan-as-you-go approach. You may want to cut and audition a few blocks at each step before committing to a particular block pattern or color or fabric combination. If you want your background blocks to form distinct subordinate patterns, a detailed sketch may be necessary. But try doing a small piece using the select-make-audition method before you say "I can't work this way." The process is liberating, goes quickly, and almost always results in a pleasing quilt.

Cutting and Construction

The background blocks are all simple to cut and assemble; quick-cutting information is provided with the menu on page 9. Templates for the shapes that can't be quick-cut appear on page 10. Watch for opportunities to use quick triangle-piecing techniques, strip-piecing methods, or other shortcuts from your own arsenal of tricks. Quick-piecing methods are efficient if you're working with a small selection of fabrics and arranging the pieces in a repetitive fashion, but impractical if you're drawing from the scrap bag or want fabric placement to be more random.

While standard block-cutting and piecing information is not included as part of this book (refer to a good basic reference, such as *The Joy of Quilting* by Joan Hanson and Mary Hickey, if you need help with fundamentals), stitching tips for a couple of the trickier units have been included on page 11.

It's important to remember that 4" is the *finished* size of the background blocks. The individual background blocks should measure 4½" from raw edge to raw edge. This is easily checked with the 4½" lines on one of your cutting rulers.

Templates and the quick-cut measurements given allow for ¼" seams. Test your seam allowance before you start your quilt:

1. From scraps, cut 3 strips, each exactly 2" wide and about 6" long. Join the strips as shown and press seams as you normally do, either open or to one side.
2. Measure the center strip. It should measure exactly 1½" wide. If it doesn't, adjust your needle position or seam guide and try again.

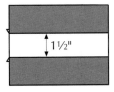

Seam 2" strips and
measure the center.

Even if you are sewing an accurate ¼" seam, the blocks with more seams may come out smaller than the blocks with fewer seams. Check your blocks occasionally to see that they are 4½" square and adjust your seam widths if necessary.

Quick-cut pieces may differ slightly in size from template-cut pieces. Again, check occasionally to see that all your blocks are 4½" square.

If you're working in true utility-quilt fashion, off-sized blocks can simply be made to fit. Blocks that are oversized can be chopped down; strips or wedges can be added to blocks that are too small or not quite square.

Because these quilts lend themselves to all-over quilting patterns, you might want to consider pressing the seams of the background blocks open, rather than to one side. This method produces less bulk, making allover quilting designs easier to execute. Many quiltmakers press seams open with no adverse results; others are uncomfortable breaking the standard "press-to-the-dark-side" rule. It is purely a matter of personal preference. If you plan to press seams open, set your stitch length to a minimum of 12 stitches per inch.

Block, Fabric, and Color Choices

The background blocks you select at each step, and the way you choose to arrange your fabrics and colors as you construct the background blocks, will affect the look of the quilt.

For a scrappy, informal quilt, you might use more fabrics, more colors, and a larger selection of background block patterns as you proceed through the steps. Though the overall layout may be balanced and symmetrical, these quilts have a generally random look. Fabrics and colors may be randomly arranged within the blocks, and the blocks themselves placed casually— sometimes right side up, sometimes sideways, sometimes upside down. The degree of contrast may vary considerably across the surface of the quilt. Some of the background blocks might be high in contrast, featuring just light and dark values; others might be done in low-contrast combinations.

For a more placid, sophisticated quilt, you might use a smaller selection of background block patterns and choose Row 1 and Row 2 blocks that

seem to go together. Limit your fabric selection to a small, coordinated group and arrange the fabrics, values, or colors in an orderly, repetitive fashion within the background blocks. Low contrast, achieved by combining fabrics that are close in color, value, or texture, softens the edges and counters the busyness of the background blocks. Shapes that are significantly lighter or darker in value will appear to float on a low-contrast background—an effect you can either avoid or exploit.

I see "Coyote Christmas" (page 77) as a rather formal quilt, despite its winsome theme; the color, value, and layout are tightly controlled. "Jordan's Quilt" (page 87) is more casual. To me, "Japanese Medallion" (page 69), "Starflight" (page 74), and "Autumn Compass" (page 77) look formal; "Televangelists" (page 74), "Ross's Quilt" (page 79), and "Watermelon Time" (page 82) look casual. We all see with a different eye: Would you classify them the same way? What about "January Nights" (page 71)? The maker used many different fabrics and a variety of background-block patterns. The degree of contrast varies considerably in the background blocks. These are casual features, but the quilt has a sophisticated look. Do you suppose it's because the colors are limited to blue, blue, and blue?

Repetition of some elements will unify the surface of the quilt, regardless of the look you're trying to achieve. Repeat a shape, color, or fabric. You might want to select a fabric or two to deliberately repeat throughout the background blocks—perhaps a nondescript neutral to pull together a scrap-bag quilt. A standout color or print will add a fleck of excitement to the more subdued pieces; accent colors and color surprises are often reserved for the Row 2 blocks, where the pieces are smaller and there are more placement options within the block itself.

As a general rule, the larger your quilt, the more variety it can sustain. Larger quilts can tolerate more fabrics, more colors, and a wider assortment of background blocks.

If you're working with extremely heavy or very delicate fabrics that are not amenable to being cut and stitched in small pieces, consider using only Row 1 blocks in your quilt.

Step by Step through the Background Blocks

Once you've decided on a blueprint and a theme, made your theme blocks, and assembled your fabrics—not necessarily in that order—it's time to put your theme block(s) on the design wall and start making background blocks.

Remember, each blueprint has a different set of rules for the 4" blocks. The number of steps, and the number of background blocks to be made at each step, varies according to the plan. Background blocks for the smaller quilts—Blueprints 1 through 5—are made in just three or four steps; the larger quilts are done in five steps.

We'll use Blueprint 7 (page 44) as an example as we discuss the select-make-audition steps for the background blocks. Later, we'll take you step by step through the decision-making process that went into the creation of "White Hemstitch," a smaller, Blueprint 5 quilt.

Blueprint 7 is based on an 8 x 10 grid, which results in a 32" x 40" quilt (without borders). The theme area is 20 squares; 60 background blocks are required to complete the quilt. The background blocks are made in five distinct steps.

Step 1: Select and make a set of 4" blocks from Row 1 of the menu.

In Blueprint 7, Step 1 calls for 24 blocks from Row 1. From the menu, select one or more of the block designs from Row 1 and make a total of 24 background blocks. Try to reflect the character of your theme block(s) by using fabrics, shapes, or colors that appear in the theme.

Often, a single block pattern is used for all of the Row 1 blocks in the first set; you can use more than one pattern if you wish. These blocks can be made up as repeat blocks, with the same fabrics, colors, or values in the same position in all the blocks; or they can be scrappy, using a mixture of fabrics randomly selected and

arranged. You might want to work with all the fabrics you've assembled, or pull out two or three to use in all the Row 1 blocks of this first set.

Repeat-fabric blocks

Repeat-color blocks

Repeat-value blocks

Random, scrappy blocks

Perhaps you've selected Block 1.6, which has two identical half-square triangle pieces, and you have decided to use a light value for one of the triangles and a dark value for the other. You'll need 48 half-square triangles to make the 24 blocks. You might select 3 of your lightest fabrics and 3 of your darkest fabrics, cutting 8 half-square triangles from each (a total of 48 triangles), and join the lights and darks at random to complete the 24 blocks. You might decide to repeat a single fabric for all of the light triangles and use the same color, but 4 different fabrics, for the dark triangles. Cutting 24 triangles from the light fabric and 6 triangles from each of the dark fabrics will give you the 48 triangles needed to make the 24 blocks.

Remember that a neutral (white, black, gray, brown, tan, ivory, taupe) can substitute for any fabric, adding interest without changing the color scheme. Perhaps you've decided to combine only dark blues and reds in your first set of Row 1 blocks. Consider substituting a black for the blue in one or two of the blocks, or a rusty brown for the red. (Read more about the role of neutrals and naturals in "Choosing Fabrics to Support Your Theme" on page 18.)

When you've cut and stitched the first set of background blocks, put the blocks on the design wall with your theme block(s). You can start arranging your blocks now, as I did with "White Hemstitch" (page 27), or you can wait until you've completed the first set of Row 2 blocks. Usually, I just plop the Row 1 blocks on the design wall willy-nilly (some touching the theme block and some at a distance) and use what I see to help me decide which Row 2 block (or blocks) I want to make in the next step.

Step 2: Select, make, and audition a set of 4" blocks from Row 2 of the menu.

In Blueprint 7, Step 2 calls for 16 blocks from Row 2. From the menu, select one or more of the 4" block designs from Row 2 and make a total of 16 background blocks.

Again, you can choose a single block pattern or more than one. If I've used a Row 1 block that's made from triangles, I usually pick a block composed primarily of squares or rectangles for my first set of Row 2 blocks—and vice versa. For a coordinated, balanced look, you could choose a Row 2 block that "goes with" or complements the Row 1 blocks you've already made.

You may want to repeat some of the fabrics and/or colors used in the Row 1 blocks and add a few more. Repetition of a fabric or color will help unify the surface of the quilt. Row 2 blocks are a good place to bring in standout fabrics, accent colors, echoes and shadows, or color surprises. Perhaps you've selected Block 2.3, a sixteen-patch. One or two of the pieces of each block could be an accent fabric, and another one or two an echo or shadow, placed either repetitively, in the same position in each block, or at random.

Once you've made your Row 2 blocks, work with your theme and background blocks on the design wall, moving things around until a pleasing

composition starts to form. Remember, you can lay out your quilt either horizontally or vertically, and you can place the theme block(s) anywhere on the grid.

I start by arranging similar blocks in columns, checkerboards, diagonal rows, clusters, or full or partial frames as shown in the examples below (rotate the page for more options). You might want to experiment with a random arrangement or try a deliberately asymmetrical layout, weighting the design to one side or corner of the quilt.

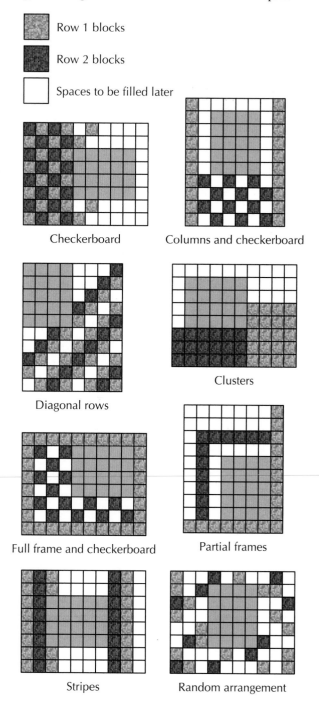

■ Row 1 blocks

■ Row 2 blocks

□ Spaces to be filled later

Checkerboard

Columns and checkerboard

Diagonal rows

Clusters

Full frame and checkerboard

Partial frames

Stripes

Random arrangement

Elements that stand out, such as accent colors or high-contrast blocks, may have to be treated in an organized way, either grouped or distributed evenly across the surface of the quilt. Blocks made up in low-contrast fabric combinations and plain 4" squares usually can be placed more randomly; they tend to sit back quietly, giving the eye a place to rest.

At this stage, you may not have enough of either of your sets of 4" blocks to form complete frames, columns, or checkerboards. You can fill in any gaps in these organized shapes when you reach the next Row 1 or Row 2 step, or you can use the filler blocks provided for in each plan. If you have more of a particular block than you need right now, set the extras aside and work them in later.

As you compose your quilt, you'll also need to consider the orientation of the individual background blocks. The blocks can be placed uniformly (all aiming the same direction), pinned up completely at random with some pointing one direction and others pointing another, or arranged to form distinct secondary patterns.

Block 1.6

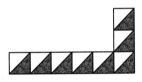

Uniform arrangement

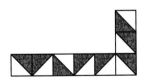

Random arrangement

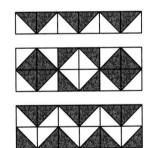

Arranged to form
secondary patterns

However you choose to arrange and orient your blocks, stay within the grid. If your plan is based on an 8 x 10 grid, your quilt should be laid out inside an area that is eight 4" blocks across and ten down, or, if you decide to work horizontally rather than vertically, ten blocks across and eight down.

Step 3: Select, make, and audition a second set of 4" blocks from Row 1 of the menu.

In Blueprint 7, Step 3 calls for 8 blocks from Row 1. You can repeat the block you made in the first set of Row 1 blocks, select an entirely different block, or repeat some and make some new. Remember, the larger your quilt, the more variety it can sustain. Larger quilts can tolerate more fabrics, more colors, and a wider variety of background blocks.

Don't be surprised if the quilt starts to dictate your choices—it may select the second set of Row 1 blocks by itself. Perhaps there is a frame or column forming that needs to be completed. Maybe the background blocks have started to organize themselves into an interesting secondary pattern that you want to pursue.

You may find that a particular color, value, or shape needs to be repeated or counterbalanced. Could you use more diagonals to balance an overabundance of horizontals and verticals? Does the quilt need to be calmed down, perhaps by using plain squares rather than pieced blocks? Do you need to tie your existing blocks together by making some transitional or "bridge" blocks, repeating at least one fabric from each of your first two sets of blocks?

Maybe you need more red, or have enough red and need to leave it out of the next set of blocks. Is it time to bring in a neutral or natural? Do you need more visual texture—prints different in pattern or scale from those you've already used?

The work that has gone before will influence the choices you make. Let the quilt help you decide; then make the new Row 1 blocks, add them to the blocks already on the design wall, and rearrange as needed.

Step 4: Select, make, and audition a second set of 4" blocks from Row 2 of the menu.

In Blueprint 7, Step 4 calls for 8 blocks from Row 2. Again, you can repeat the block you made in the first set of Row 2 blocks, select an entirely different block, or repeat some and make some new.

By this time, the quilt may be totally out of your control. It may leave you no choice but to complete it with a particular Row 2 block, crafted from particular colors or fabrics. If it is very strong-willed, it might insist that you abandon your original plan. Sometimes, a quilt based on a 7 x 9 grid will demand 8 x 8 medallion status or decide it wants to be 6 x 9 or 7 x 10. It may refuse to accept any more Row 2 blocks. It might even reject its theme block and demand a replacement. This is a time to be flexible! Be prepared to depart from the rules for the good of the quilt.

Step 5: Select and make the filler blocks.

If your quilt is well behaved, letting you complete Step 4 without seizing control of its design, you're ready to complete the quilt with filler blocks. Blueprint 7 calls for 4 filler blocks. These can be any block from any row: something you've already used, something new, or a combination—whatever is required to complete the quilt. Usually, filler blocks are used to complete frames, columns, checkerboards, or other organized patterns that have developed on the design wall in the earlier steps.

Put these last background blocks on the design wall and take a good look at your quilt. It might require some minor tinkering. Look for "soft spots" and "black holes"—areas that may be either too weak or too strong in relation to the rest of the surface. Is the color distribution pleasing? Are the patterns and shapes defined (or obscured) to your satisfaction? You may need to rearrange the elements, or rotate some of the background blocks if unwanted secondary patterns have formed. Don't hesitate to redo or replace any background blocks that simply refuse to work.

If something looks terribly wrong, it may be that the theme block has ceased to coexist with the background, suddenly looking as if it belongs to an entirely different quilt. The fastest and often most successful solution is to dip into your fabric stash and pull out some wonderful pieces that fit the color scheme and the look of the background blocks; audition these in place of the original theme. A special fabric that you've loved (and perhaps hoarded) is often just what is needed to pull the pieces together. The reject—that carefully chosen theme block that no longer works —can eventually be used in a different quilt.

COMPLETING THE QUILT

Framing the Theme Blocks

If your theme blocks need to be framed, either to make them fit their assigned spaces or as a deliberate design choice, now is the time to decide on the colors and fabrics to use and complete the frames (see "Sizing Things Up" on page 15).

If frames no longer seem appropriate to the quilt, you can fill the gaps with full or partial background blocks. If you do frame the theme blocks, remember that the sizes given with the blueprints are finished sizes; be sure to allow for seams!

Assembling the Quilt

When the composition on the design wall suits you and all the holes are filled, you're ready to assemble the pieces into a quilt. Because theme areas vary in size, shape, and placement, the quilts usually cannot be stitched together by rows. Some of the background blocks may need to be joined into squares or rectangles before they can be properly attached to their neighboring theme blocks.

Sometimes, in the process of moving the blocks from the design wall to the sewing machine, things get confused, especially if you're chain stitching. No matter how careful you are, some blocks get turned sideways or end up stitched to the wrong side of another block. The best way to keep things straight is to take a photo with a Polaroid camera before you start removing blocks from the design wall. If an instant camera isn't available, snip a tiny triangle from the upper left-hand corner of each block while all the elements are safely attached to the design wall. This gives you a permanent "this side up" indicator, which helps considerably.

Some quilters trim or square up their blocks before they assemble them into a quilt. Trimming is risky business, and it shouldn't be needed if your pieces have been accurately cut and stitched.

4. The Second Set of Row 1 Blocks

Step 3 calls for 8 more blocks from Row 1. After I placed the Row 2 blocks, I found I had 8 empty spaces adjoining the theme block—the logical position for the next set of Row 1 blocks. I wanted to emphasize the green diamond shape that I had built with the first set of Row 1 blocks, so I made 8 more green-and-light half-square triangle blocks and auditioned them with the rest of the quilt.

These simple half-square triangle blocks worked pretty well, but I decided I could do better. As I studied the layout and the quilt, the corner of the theme block caught my eye. It occurred to me that filling the 8 blanks with this corner design—a Row 1 variation—might be just what the quilt needed (see "Background Variations" on pages 61–62).

Row 1
variation

5. The Fillers

Step 4 calls for 4 filler blocks—whatever is needed to complete the quilt. The only unfilled spaces left were the outside corners. I tried filling these with the unused half-square triangle blocks from the previous step, but decided that the quilt would "finish off" better if I used 4 of the Row 1 variation blocks, which I quickly made and placed. Satisfied, I started rummaging for border fabrics.

Row 1
variation

6. Borders and Finishing

I didn't have enough of any of the fabrics I'd used in the body of the quilt for borders or binding. A green-and-black stripe from my stash seemed to work well as a narrow inner border. The large-scale, tone-on-tone pink print for the outer border required another trip to the quilt shop. This border started out much wider; I gradually chopped it down until the width looked right. If I were doing it again, I might not chop quite so much!

The quilt was hand quilted with pink #12 perle cotton. Most of the background quilting is done in straight lines, emphasizing the diamond medallion. A scalloped circle appears in the center of the quilt, and the border quilting includes both gentle curves and straight lines.

Blueprints for Creative Quilts

Quick Reference Chart

Blueprint	Finished Size Without Borders	Grid	Theme Area	Theme Block Possibilities
1	16" x 20"	4 x 5	4 squares	One 8" block *or* Four 4" blocks
2	24" x 24"	6 x 6	9 squares	One 12" block *or* Two 8" and one 4" block
3	24" x 32"	6 x 8	12 squares	One 12" and three 4" blocks *or* Two 8" and four 4" blocks *or* Three 8" blocks *or* One 12" x 16" rectangle
4	28" x 36"	7 x 9	16 squares	One 16" block *or* One 12", one 8", and three 4" blocks *or* Three 8" and four 4" blocks *or* Four 8" blocks
5	32" x 32"	8 x 8	16 squares	Same as Blueprint 4
6	32" x 36"	8 x 9	18 squares	One 16" and two 4" blocks *or* Two 12" blocks *or* One 12" x 24" rectangle
7	32" x 40"	8 x 10	20 squares	One 16" and one 8" block *or* One 16" and four 4" blocks *or* Two 12" and two 4" blocks *or* Four 8" and four 4" blocks *or* Five 8" blocks *or* One 16" x 20" rectangle

BLUEPRINT	FINISHED SIZE WITHOUT BORDERS	GRID	THEME AREA	THEME BLOCK POSSIBILITIES
8	32" x 44"	8 x 11	22 squares	One 16", one 8", and two 4" blocks *or* Two 12" and one 8" block *or* Two 12" and four 4" blocks
9	32" x 48"	8 x 12	24 squares	One 16" and two 8" blocks *or* One 16", one 8", and four 4" blocks *or* Two 12", one 8", and two 4" blocks *or* Five 8" and four 4" blocks *or* Six 8" blocks *or* One 12" x 32" rectangle *or* One 16" x 24" rectangle
10	36" x 36"	9 x 9	20 squares	Same as Blueprint 7
11	36" x 48"	9 x 12	27 squares	One 16", one 12", and two 4" blocks *or* One 16", two 8", and three 4" blocks *or* Three 12" blocks *or* Two 12", two 8", and one 4" block *or* One 12" x 36" rectangle
12	40" x 40"	10 x 10	25 squares	One 20" block *or* One 16" and one 12" block *or* Two 12", one 8", and three 4" blocks *or* Five 8" and five 4" blocks

Blueprint 1

4 x 5 grid
16" x 20" without borders
Theme area: 4 squares

16 background blocks
(see "The Menu" on pages 8–9):
    Step 1: 8 from Row 1
    Step 2: 4 from Row 2
    Step 3: 4 fillers

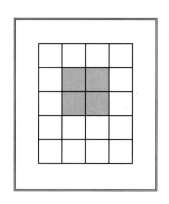

Blueprint 1A
One 8" theme block

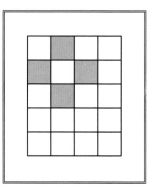

Blueprint 1B
Four 4" theme blocks

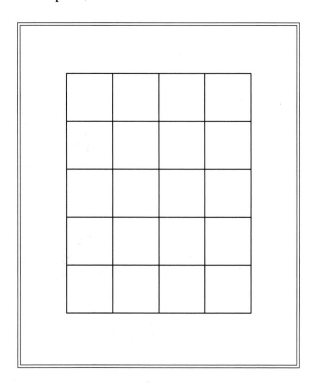

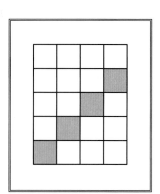

**Blueprint 1B
variation**

1 square = 4"

All sizes given are finished sizes; allow for seams.

Shaded areas suggest theme placement,
but theme blocks may be placed anywhere
within the grid.

For a horizontal quilt, rotate the blueprint 90°.

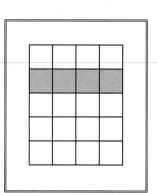

Blueprint 1C
4-square theme area

MARTHA WASHINGTON STAR

by Judy Dafoe Hopkins, 1997, Anchorage, Alaska, 19" x 20¼".
Judy used three solids in an Amish palette and just two 4" block designs (1.7 and 2.9, see pages 8–9) for this simple little quilt, which features a traditional pieced Martha Washington Star block as the theme. The major design elements appear to float above a dark surface, a result of using the same fabric for the background in all the blocks. The quilt has narrow borders on two sides and is hand quilted with straight lines, diagonal grids, and "punkin seed" motifs.

Blueprint 2

6 x 6 grid
24" x 24" without borders
Theme area: 9 squares

27 background blocks
(see "The Menu" on pages 8–9):
    Step 1: 12 from Row 1
    Step 2: 6 from Row 2
    Step 3: 6 from Row 1
    Step 4: 3 fillers

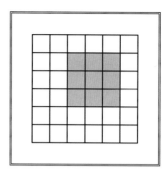

Blueprint 2A
One 12" theme block

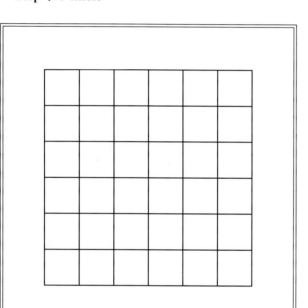

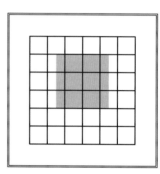

**Blueprint 2A
variation**

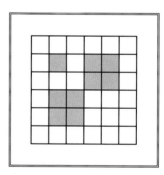

Blueprint 2B
Two 8" and one 4"
theme blocks

1 square = 4"

All sizes given are finished sizes; allow for seams.

Shaded areas suggest theme placement,
but theme blocks may be placed anywhere
within the grid.

Theme blocks can be centered by splitting
some of the background blocks.

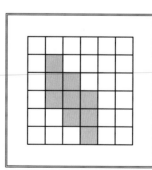

Blueprint 2C
9-square theme area

Blueprints

by Judy Dafoe Hopkins, 1997, Anchorage, Alaska, 26¾" x 26¾".
This quilt was made from the front and back sides of just one fabric: a long jacket with a cyanotyped leaf-and-branch design that hung unused in Judy's closet because it was too nice to wear. The half-square triangle blocks (Block 1.6) are alternately turned to form a striking outer frame. Narrow borders and front-turned-to-back binding complete the quilt. The piece is quilted with contrasting perle cotton and larger-than-normal stitches for a sashiko look; the checkerboard area is crow-footed (see page 26).

Blueprint 3

6 x 8 grid
24" x 32" without borders
Theme area: 12 squares

36 background blocks
(see "The Menu" on pages 8–9):
Step 1: 16 from Row 1
Step 2: 8 from Row 2
Step 3: 8 from Row 1
Step 4: 4 fillers

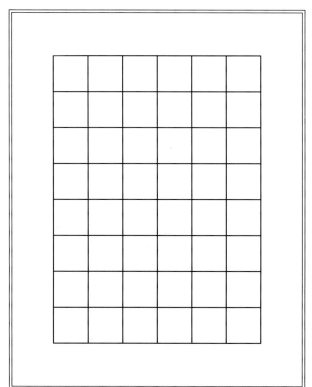

1 square = 4"

All sizes given are finished sizes; allow for seams.

Shaded areas suggest theme placement,
but theme blocks may be placed anywhere
within the grid.

For a horizontal quilt, rotate the blueprint 90°.

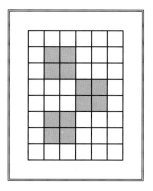

Blueprint 3A
Three 8" theme blocks

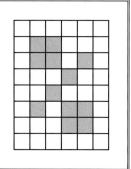

Blueprint 3B
Four 4" and two 8"
theme blocks

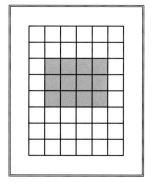

Blueprint 3C
One 12" x 16"
theme block

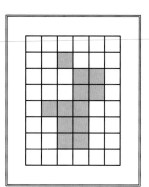

Blueprint 3D
12-square theme area

Nighty-Night

by Dee Morrow, 1997, Anchorage, Alaska, 45" x 50".

Dee designed and appliquéd the theme blocks for this charming quilt. The moon's features are embroidered; the poem is hand printed with silver pen ("It takes a little practice," says Dee). Two blue prints, close in color and value but different in visual texture, are used as background throughout—a pleasing backdrop for the cheerful red, yellow, and turquoise squares and triangles. The background-block arrangement is random. Repetitive use of the red-and-white striped fabric in the theme blocks and the pinwheels (Block 2.7) unifies the surface of the quilt; 6" Pinwheel blocks anchor two of the border corners.

Blueprint 7

8 x 10 grid
32" x 40" without borders
Theme area: 20 squares

60 background blocks
(see "The Menu" on pages 8–9):
   Step 1: 24 from Row 1
   Step 2: 16 from Row 2
   Step 3: 8 from Row 1
   Step 4: 8 from Row 2
   Step 5: 4 fillers

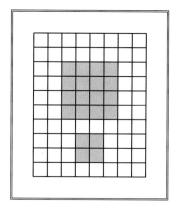

Blueprint 7A
One 8" and one 16"
theme blocks

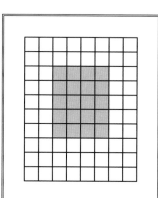

Blueprint 7B
16" x 20" theme block

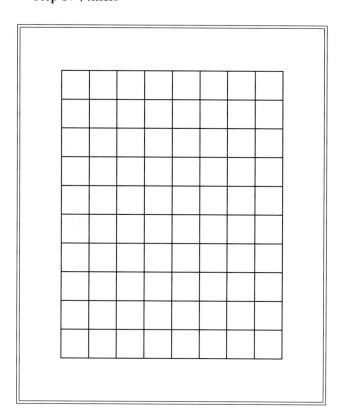

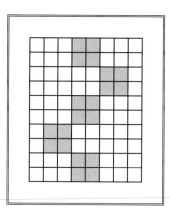

Blueprint 7C
Five 8" theme blocks

1 square = 4"

All sizes given are finished sizes; allow for seams.

Shaded areas suggest theme placement,
but theme blocks may be placed anywhere
within the grid.

For a horizontal quilt, rotate the blueprint 90°.

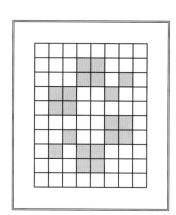

Blueprint 7D
Four 4" and four 8"
theme blocks

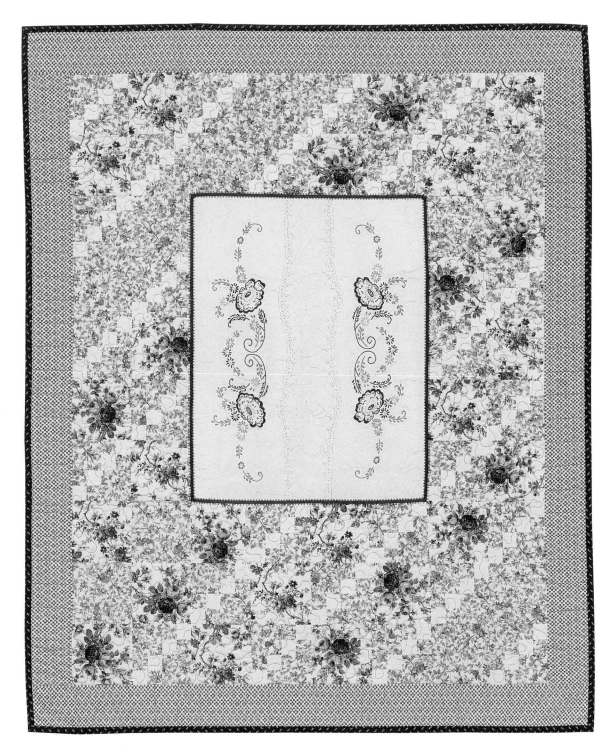

Love As Ever

by Ruth Strickling and Judy Dafoe Hopkins, 1997, Anchorage, Alaska, 36½" x 44¼".
Judy used a pair of pillowcases embroidered by her Aunt Ruth as the theme for this romantic quilt; the hand-crocheted edging remains intact. All of the Row 1 blocks are plain 4" squares (Block 1.1) cut from two different floral fabrics—one a large-scale print and the other smaller in scale. Row 1 and Row 2 blocks are laid out in diagonal rows; the small white-on-white squares in the Row 2 blocks (Block 2.4) form delicate chains. The green checked border fabric serves as counterpoint. Picot-edged red ribbon, applied after the piece was quilted, picks up the color of the embroidered flowers. Quilted by Kathy Mosher with metallic threads.

Blueprint 8

8 x 11 grid
32" x 44" without borders
Theme area: 22 squares

66 background blocks
(see "The Menu" on pages 8–9):
    Step 1: 30 from Row 1
    Step 2: 16 from Row 2
    Step 3: 8 from Row 1
    Step 4: 8 from Row 2
    Step 5: 4 fillers

Possibilities

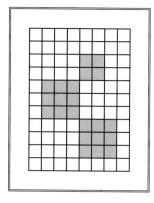

Blueprint 8A
One 8" and two 12"
theme blocks

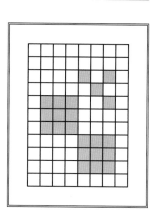

**Blueprint 8A
variation**

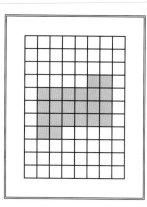

Blueprint 8B
Four 4" and two 12"
theme blocks

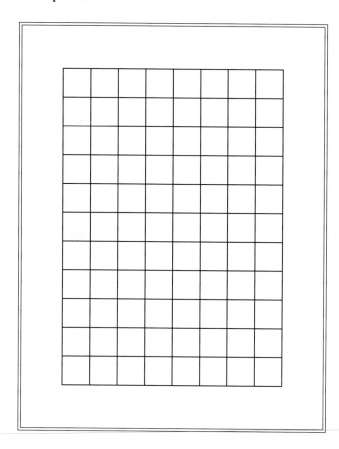

1 square = 4"

All sizes given are finished sizes; allow for seams.

Shaded areas suggest theme placement,
but theme blocks may be placed anywhere
within the grid.

For a horizontal quilt, rotate the blueprint 90°.

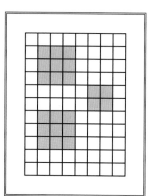

Blueprint 8C
22-square theme area

ALL GOOD POSSUMS GO TO HEAVEN

by Terri Shinn, 1997, Snohomish, Washington, 51½" x 65".

This piece is Terri's gentle statement about road kill: "I feel so sorry for the poor ugly possums and know their mothers think that all good possums go to heaven." Here, an angelic appliquéd possum floats serenely through a celestial forest; the tree shapes are rendered in plaids, stripes, and other unusual fabrics from Terri's eclectic collection. Striped fabrics, arranged both horizontally and vertically, underlie the whimsical multicolored words appliquéd in the border.

Blueprint 9

8 x 12 grid
32" x 48" without borders
Theme area: 24 squares

72 background blocks
(see "The Menu" on pages 8–9):
    Step 1: 32 from Row 1
    Step 2: 20 from Row 2
    Step 3: 8 from Row 1
    Step 4: 8 from Row 2
    Step 5: 4 fillers

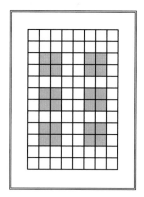

Blueprint 9A
Six 8" theme blocks

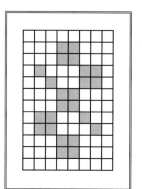

Blueprint 9B
Four 4" and five 8"
theme blocks

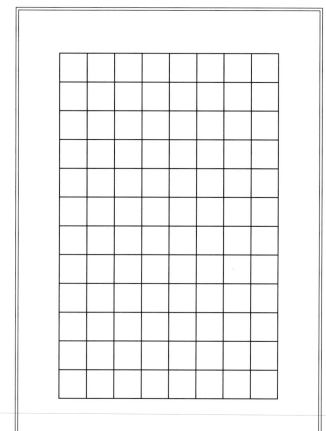

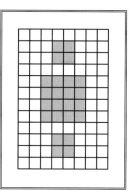

Blueprint 9C
Two 8" and one 16"
theme blocks

1 square = 4"

All sizes given are finished sizes; allow for seams.

Shaded areas suggest theme placement,
but theme blocks may be placed anywhere
within the grid.

For a horizontal quilt, rotate the blueprint 90°.

Blueprint 9D
16" x 24" theme block

THE SISTERHOOD

by Jacquelin Carley, 1997, Anchorage, Alaska, 44" x 60".

This quilt has a painterly look. Scenes from a pictorial print depicting early Indian life serve as the theme. Jackie heightened the impact of the smaller theme blocks with careful placement of the light triangles in the surrounding background blocks. The higher-contrast background blocks are arranged to form distinct secondary designs. Southwest Indian motifs, quilted in metallic thread in the border, include the bear paw and the turtle; the turtle represents the power of women and is believed to protect women in childbirth.

Blueprint 10

9 x 9 grid
36" x 36" without borders
Theme area: 20 squares

61 background blocks
(see "The Menu" on pages 8–9):
    Step 1: 24 from Row 1
    Step 2: 16 from Row 2
    Step 3: 8 from Row 1
    Step 4: 8 from Row 2
    Step 5: 5 fillers

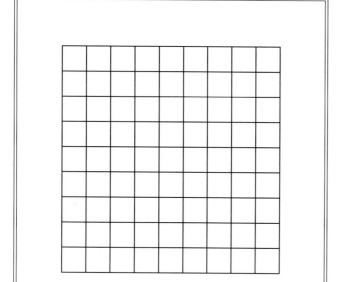

1 square = 4"

All sizes given are finished sizes; allow for seams.

Shaded areas suggest theme placement, but theme blocks may be placed anywhere within the grid.

Possibilities

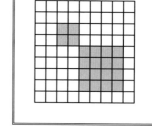

Blueprint 10A
One 8" and one 16" theme blocks

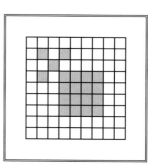

Blueprint 10B
Four 4" and one 16" theme blocks

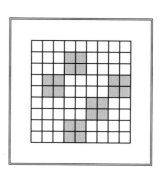

Blueprint 10C
Five 8" theme blocks

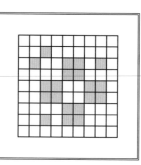

Blueprint 10D
Four 4" and four 8" theme blocks

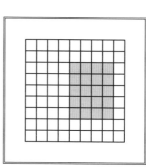

Blueprint 10E
16" x 20" theme block

POSIES IN A ROW

by Kathy Mosher, 1997, Anchorage, Alaska, 49" x 49".

Kathy floated her five traditional Cake Stand blocks on a subtle background that combines light-to-medium gradation with a watercolor look. Two of the Cake Stands are obvious, the other three obscured. Broderie perse flowers, fused and outlined in a machine blanket stitch with metallic thread, spill from the baskets. The background blocks (1.1, 1.7, and 2.4) are arranged in diagonal rows; the main border fabric is a sumptuous, large-scale floral print with a copper-colored metallic background. Machine stippling and large trapunto roses complete the quilt.

Blueprint 11

9 x 12 grid
36" x 48" without borders
Theme area: 27 squares

81 background blocks
(see "The Menu" on pages 8–9):
    Step 1: 36 from Row 1
    Step 2: 20 from Row 2
    Step 3: 10 from Row 1
    Step 4: 10 from Row 2
    Step 5: 5 fillers

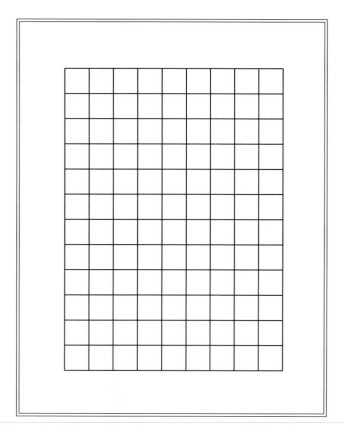

1 square = 4"

All sizes given are finished sizes; allow for seams.

Shaded areas suggest theme placement, but theme blocks may be placed anywhere within the grid.

For a horizontal quilt, rotate the blueprint 90°.

Possibilities

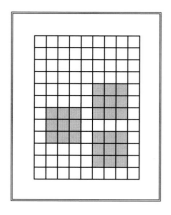

Blueprint 11A
Three 12" theme blocks

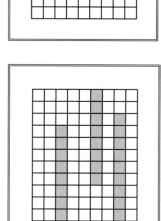

Blueprint 11B
12" x 36" theme block

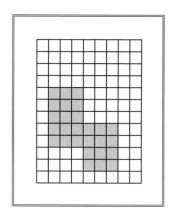

Blueprint 11C
27-square theme area

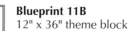

**Blueprint 11C
variation**

2", 3", and 6" Background Blocks

Following are cutting measurements for 2", 3", and 6" background blocks. Templates are provided on pages 90–92.

For 2" background blocks:
A—2½" square
B—1½" x 2½" rectangle
C—Use template.
D—1" x 2½" rectangle
E—1½" square
F—Divided 2⅞" square yields 2.

G—Twice-divided 3¼" square yields 4.

H—Use template.
J—Use template.
K—Divided 1⅞" square yields 2.

L—Use template.
M—1" square
N—Use template.
P—Use template.

For 3" background blocks:
A—3½" square
B—2" x 3½" rectangle
C—1½" x 3½" rectangle
D—1¼" x 3½" rectangle
E—2" square
F—Divided 3⅞" square yields 2.

G—Twice-divided 4¼" square yields 4.

H—Use template.
J—Use template.
K—Divided 2⅜" square yields 2.

L—1½" square
M—1¼" square
N—2⅝" square
P—1⁹⁄₁₆" square (halfway between 1½" and 1⅝" on your ruler)

For 6" background blocks:
A—6½" square
B—3½" x 6½" rectangle
C—2½" x 6½" rectangle
D—2" x 6½" rectangle
E—3½" square
F—Divided 6⅞" square yields 2.

G—Twice-divided 7¼" square yields 4.

H—Use template.
J—Use template.
K—Divided 3⅞" square yields 2.

L—2½" square
M—2" square
N—4¾" square
P—2⅝" square

LAYOUT VARIATIONS

In early framed-center quilts, the background blocks are sometimes set on point, even when the central block is set straight. This is a variation worth experimenting with if you're not satisfied with the look of your quilt in a conventional layout or if you're using on-point theme blocks.

In "Coyote Christmas" (page 77), all of the blocks are set on point. To take advantage of the Southwest-motif print, the theme blocks were cut as on-point squares. If I had added triangles to the corners to make the blocks sit square, they would have been too large to fit my grid and too clunky for the quilt I envisioned. Putting everything on point was the logical solution.

Many charming old-time utility quilts feature scrap centers surrounded by sprightly appliquéd borders, like the illustration below. This format is certainly appropriate for a One-of-a-Kind quilt: fill the center of the quilt with background blocks (perhaps your rejects or leftovers?) and let the border carry the theme. In the illustration, the theme in the border obviously occupies more than 25% of the quilt's surface—but we all know by now that that's just fine!

Variations in Approach

While continuing to rely on the basic One-of-a-Kind framework, many quiltmakers choose to rearrange the steps, making background blocks first and adding theme blocks that suit the background later. Others challenge themselves to create distinctive quilt surfaces while staying within the parameters of the basic blueprint. Susan Roberts planned "Alpine Meadow" on paper before she started to cut and sew. Working from Blueprint 7, Susan started by creating rectangular theme blocks with curved lines that would form soft hills. She totaled the number of Row 1 and Row 2 blocks available to her under the blueprint, selected blocks that could be organized into tree and mountain images, and arranged and rearranged them in pencil until her inviting scene emerged. Executing the quilt in fabrics she dyed herself, Susan extended forms and colors used in the body of the quilt into the borders and binding.

Preliminary planning may be required if you want to develop a particular background design, as in "Evan's Eloquent Equine" (page 73) or "Stars and Stripes" (page 82); an elegant landscape, such as "Mountain Memories" (page 76); or an irregularly shaped quilt, as in "Native Horse" (page 81). It's okay to get out the graph paper on occasions like these!

Many quilters have adapted the One-of-a-Kind method to fit their personal styles and needs. Judy Morningstar says: "I don't follow the recipes exactly. I make heaps of background blocks of every kind and use them where they look best. Not because I don't think it's a good system—it's just that I never do what I am told!"

Linda Flanders, by nature a designer and planner, gives herself permission to relax and play: "In the early stages, I have to fight my desire to control the piece. I just arrange the units as well as I can, knowing that I can always make changes later. I don't force myself into using only the units made during the book's suggested steps. I allow myself the freedom to make extra units and to keep changing the arrangement of units until I feel good about the layout. I allow myself to change the original plan and to make changes to the theme block. I allow myself as much time as I need, and I use the steps in the book as guidelines, not rules."

The One-of-a-Kind process is simply a springboard to the creation of quilts that carry a personal imprint. The blueprints, the menu, and the method provide structure and direction—a starting point. Use what is useful, but feel free to detour or take another path. As the King of Hearts told the White Rabbit: "Begin at the beginning and go on till you come to the end; then stop."[7] In the wonderland of One-of-a-Kind quilts, there really are only two rules: Enjoy the process, and take pleasure in the result.

Alpine Meadow
by Susan E. Roberts, 1988, Wasilla, Alaska, 52½" x 45".

A Gallery of Creative Quilts

WHITE HEMSTITCH
by Judy Dafoe Hopkins, 1997, Anchorage, Alaska, 42½" x 42½". Quilted by Peggy Hinchey.

KINSINGER BASKET ◄

by Deb Coates, 1997,
Brush Prairie, Washington,
49″ x 49″.
Pieced baskets appliquéd to plaid
backgrounds provide the focus in this
all-wool interpretation of a quirky
1910 Basket quilt made by
Mrs. Ann Shanks of Benwell,
Newcastle-upon-Tyne.

MEMORIES IN SILK ►

by Carol Harowitz Miller,
1993, Richmond, Virginia,
36″ x 40″.
Carol coordinated the
American half of a 1993
Japan-Virginia quilt show;
this special memento is
made from a hand-painted
silk handkerchief and
kimono remnants presented
to her by the visiting
Japanese quilters.

Gallery   67

SYNCOPATED SUNRISE ▶

by Judy Dafoe Hopkins, 1997, Anchorage, Alaska, 33½" x 36½".
This quilt and "Mutt on the Monitor" (below) are the result of a mini-challenge in which two quiltmakers agreed to work with the same plan (Blueprint 4) and with half-yard cuts of exactly the same group of fabrics. Quilted by Peggy Hinchey.

MUTT ON THE MONITOR ▼

by Dee Morrow, 1996, Anchorage, Alaska, 36½" x 28½".
Dee's Blueprint 4 challenge quilt, a companion to "Syncopated Sunrise" (above), features a single theme block.

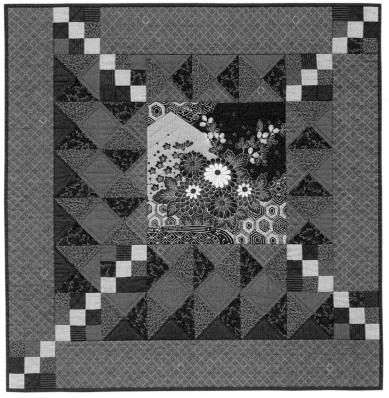

SNORKELING ▲

*by Susan Jeffers Edwards,
1994, La Canada, California,
43" x 35".*
The theme fabric—a 16"
batik panel—is framed with
two rounds of strips to fill a
20" x 20" square. (Collection
of Thomas Hazen Edwards)

JAPANESE MEDALLION ◄

*by Janet Brodie, 1992, Dobbs Ferry,
New York, 31½" x 31½".*
Janet created a striking surround
for her theme block by carefully
controlling the color placement in
the 4" quarter-square triangle blocks
(Block 1.8).

OH MY GOSH, IT'S ◄
TRADITIONAL

by Linda Flanders, 1997,
Hattiesburg, Mississippi,
38½" x 38½".
Linda integrated the traditional
Ohio Star theme block with
the background by replacing
two of the corners with pieced
background blocks (Block 1.8);
the pink-and-blue floral
squares, arranged in a diagonal
chain from bottom left to top
right, pass through the other
two corners of the theme.

STRING STAR ◄

by Judy Dafoe Hopkins, 1997,
Anchorage, Alaska, 37½" x 38".
Judy used small scraps of
authentic depression-era fabrics
from the collection of Doris
Rhodes to create the string star
and the surrounding small
checkerboards (Block 2.3); the
pink and yellow squares in the
outer frame (Block 1.5) are
reproduction prints. Quilted by
Peggy Hinchey.

RACING WITH THE WIND ◄

by Linda B. Holt, 1996, Santa Maria, California, 44" x 55 ¾".
Printed-panel sailboats and a traditional Mariner's Compass block from Judy Mathieson's book anchor this brisk quilt, made in a Sandy Turner class for Linda's husband, Nick, who loves to sail. Compare this piece with "Televangelists" (page 74); while very different, both are Blueprint 11 quilts, and the theme-block size and placement are identical.

JANUARY NIGHTS ▼

by Katheryn Russi, 1994, Rochester, Michigan, 50 ½" x 42".
Inspired by and begun during a cold, wintry January in 1994, this Blueprint 7D quilt has four 8" and four 4" theme blocks, all in the traditional Simple Star design (also known as Variable Star or Sawtooth Star). The groupings of triangles (Block 1.10) represent snow-covered trees.

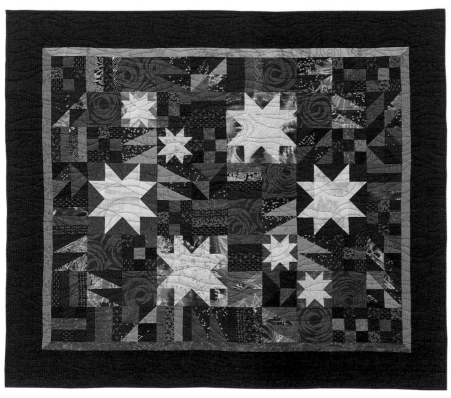

STEVE'S JUNGLE PLAYGROUND ▶

by Sandy Bartholomew, 1992, Anchorage, Alaska, 42" x 54".

Polka dots galore! It's no wonder Steve loves this quilt. The irregularly shaped theme area was expanded by two units to accommodate the appliquéd design, an enlargement of motifs in the multicolored animal print used in the background blocks. Sandy manipulated the color and orientation of her background blocks (Blocks 1.7 and 2.5) to produce a lively lattice that would make a good turnpike for toy cars or a pleasant route for a plastic-animal parade. (Collection of Steve Roundhill)

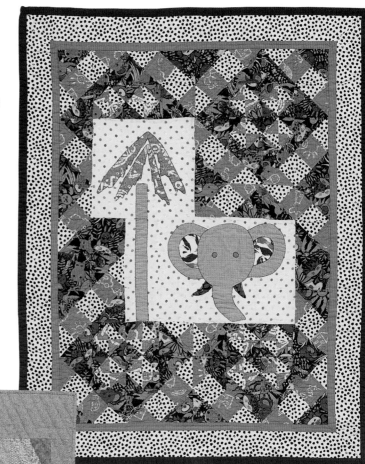

BENJAMIN'S QUILT ◀

by Martha P. Supnik, 1996, Carlisle, Massachusetts, 30" x 42".

There's a twin to this quilt—made for Benjamin's twin brother, Matthew. Martha drafted the paper-pieced letters on her computer, inspired by those in a Carol Doak book. The central triangle of the corner star is pieced into the border; the remaining triangles are faced and inserted in the seams. "It was easier than piecing the whole star," Martha says, "and I think kids like something on their quilts to fiddle with." (Collection of Marian Presberg Stolman)

SOMEBUNNIES ▶

by Sally J. Cameron, 1989, Anchorage, Alaska, 38" x 37¾".

Sally collects bunnies and bunny fabrics, many of which are included in this delightful quilt. The theme block is a pieced bunny from Debbie Mumm's *A Bunch of Bunnies* and is framed with a narrow band that sets it apart from the lively assortment of multicolored background blocks. Sally used Blocks 2.1 and 1.9 to create crisp carrots, repeating them in the borders.

LOTUS ◀

by Louise Colbert, 1997, Anchorage, Alaska, 41¼" x 41¼".

This elegant quilt features motifs cut from a printed fabric as the theme; the smaller design is reprised in the outer border.

EVAN'S ELOQUENT EQUINE ▶

by Ruth Norman, Linda Parkhouse, Sandy Bartholomew, and Julie Tillman, 1991, Anchorage, Alaska, 50" x 50".

Four friends took on the task of making One-of-a-Kind quilts for a bevy of babies born in their church in 1991. The jaunty appliquéd carousel horse was inspired by a coloring-book drawing. The organized, eye-catching background, made from Blocks 1.7 and 2.8, gives the illusion of depth. Quilted by Ruth Norman. (Collection of Kittie Rakovan)

STARFLIGHT ▶

by Judy Chaney, 1996, Windsor, California, 44½" x 44½".

A Blueprint 12 quilt that grew, Judy's sophisticated piece features a LeMoyne Star with Flying Geese designed in a Sharyn Craig class. Dark checks in the Nine Patch background blocks (Block 2.2) form chains, which occasionally interrupt the outer frame. Diagonal bands formed from Block 1.6 pull the LeMoyne Star fabric through the quilt. The remaining spaces are filled with plain 4" squares, showing the beautiful batiks to best advantage.

TELEVANGELISTS ◀

by Jeannette Tousley Muir, 1990, Moorestown, New Jersey, 43½" x 55".

"The purpose of this quilt was to use every ugly fabric in my possession, to accompany a hideous cartoon fabric given to me by my friends," Jeannette reports. Three theme blocks, the traditional Crazy House design, are surrounded by background blocks crafted in a mad mix of color and pattern. Caricatures cut from the cartoon fabric are framed in window-style blocks.

ROSS'S QUILT ◀

by Robin Benjamin, 1996, Fairbanks, Alaska, 41" x 47".

Robin used reverse appliqué panels from an "Arctic Appliqué" class to craft this cheery quilt for her son Ross. The uniformly dark background lets the figures take center stage.

JAPANESE CRANES AND APPLE BLOSSOMS ▶

by Reynola Pakusich, 1991, Bellingham, Washington, 54" x 66".

Reynola enjoys working with the One-of-a-Kind technique, which allows her to display and focus her collection of ethnic and hand-designed fabrics. This excellent example, featuring a Japanese cranes-and-blossoms print, is glorious in blacks, whites, pinks, and golds. Quilted by Barbara Ford.

by Sandy Turner, 1997, Santa Maria, California, 39½" x 48".

"Sometimes it pays to wait!" says Sandy. "I purchased the upper sailboat theme fabric two years before I found the fabric I used for the lower theme." Sandy opened up the scene and softened the lines of the pictorial fabrics' sewn edges by repeating the theme fabric in adjoining 4" blocks. Pieced boats and Snail's Trail blocks enliven the background.

ANNIVERSARY QUILT WITH IRIS ▶

by Reynola Pakusich, 1990, Bellingham, Washington, 52" x 63".

A floral decorating fabric serves as the theme for this striking quilt, a fiftieth wedding anniversary gift for Reynola's aunt and uncle. Reynola gave the delicate iris room to breathe by using 4" blocks in a color and value that closely matches the focus-fabric background. The pointy blue-and-green background blocks (Block 1.10) echo the leaf shapes in the print. (Collection of Dora and Berdell Hose)

NATIVE HORSE ▶

by Harold T. Solt and Carol Thatcher Solt, 1996, Anacortes, Washington, 36¾" x 40½".

This husband-and-wife team has been working together on fiber pieces for more than a decade: Harold does the cross-stitch, and Carol incorporates the needlework into hangings or quilts. This stunning example, crafted around a P. Buckley Moss cross-stitch pattern from June Grigg/designs, was inspired by native Chilkat blankets. "The cross-stitch (panel) was too narrow by ½", so the long strips were born," says Carol, who created the quilt to show students in her One-of-a-Kind classes that "borders and boundaries are limitless."

FROM THE PRAIRIES ◀

by Judy Morningstar, 1997, Goodlands, Manitoba, Canada, 27" x 39½".
Twin to a 1993 quilt Dr. Eamonn Twomey purchased as a gift for his mother, Dettie Twomey of County Cork, Ireland, this memento of the Canadian prairie features the United Grain Growers' elevator in Deloraine, Manitoba, as the theme. A farmer, Judy regretfully notes that grain elevators are being phased out; she feels it is important to at least preserve their images.

WATERMELON TIME ◀

by Carol Rhoades, 1996, Anchorage, Alaska, 21½″ x 17¾″.
The appliquéd bunny was inspired by a Bottman Design greeting card. Carol likes to work small; the background blocks in this piece measure 2″. Note the watermelon slices Carol created by adding a strip to the base of the J shape in Block 1.9.

LITTLE LIBERTY ▶

by M. Diane Nielsen, 1987, Longmont, Colorado, 13″ x 16″.
Diane took small scraps from each of the fifty-one winning quilts in the 1986 Liberty contest (see page 57) to create this unique piece. (Collection of Judy Dafoe Hopkins)

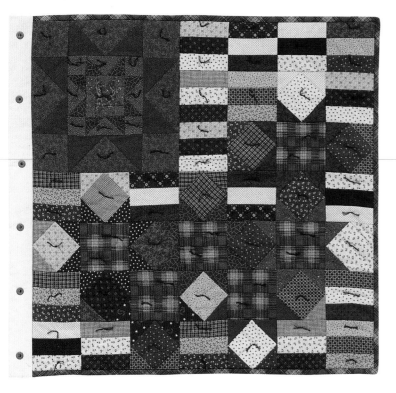

STARS AND STRIPES ◀

by Catherine Shultz, 1989, Anchorage, Alaska, 30″ x 28″.
Cathy's clever flag quilt was made in a One-of-a-Kind USA class, where participants were asked to bring a patriotic theme block and colors. The low-contrast Radiant Star theme block takes a back seat to the more obvious cluster of touching stars, created from a group of square-in-a-square background blocks (Block 2.8) with deliberate placement of the blue triangles.

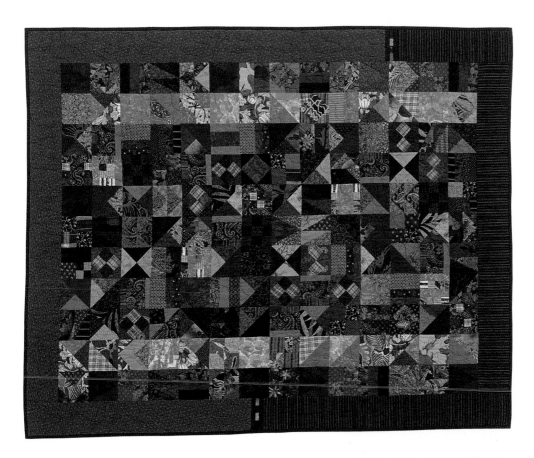

MERRY BIRTHDAY ▲

by friends of Judy Hopkins, 1991,
Anchorage, Alaska, 64½" x 53".
When the makers of the quilts for the original
One-of-a-Kind Quilts book presented Judy with a
collection of background blocks in reds, tans,
blacks, and browns, she put them together as a
scrap quilt, without a formal theme. The lighter
blocks, arranged in bars near the outside edges of
the quilt, provide a focal point.

DING DONG, THE WITCH IS DEAD ▶

by Judy Dafoe Hopkins, 1988,
Anchorage, Alaska, 44" x 51⅜".
The Kansas farmhouse and Dorothy theme blocks
are linked by a pieced brick road, with bricks sized
to accommodate the Toto print. During the
composition process, Judy realized that these major
design elements couldn't hold their own against
additional pieced background blocks. The subtle
black-and-red plaid used to fill the center and to
frame the road provided the needed contrast; two
narrow red borders fill the resulting 2" gap. The
Dorothy design is from the Quilts & Other
Comforts' "Patchwork Pals" pattern.

PURPLE IRIS ▶

by Peggy Baker Deierhoi, 1993,
Westlake, Ohio, 40" x 51½".

A pair of pretty floral prints, one dark and one light, occupy the theme area of this dynamic quilt, but the eye is drawn to the dramatic designs Peggy created with the background blocks. Quilted by Lottie Krause. (Collection of Sara Deierhoi Clark)

BLEST BE THE TIE ◀

by Ruth Fairbanks, 1996,
Sault Ste. Marie, Michigan,
34½" x 38½".

Ruth used pictures from the family album, photocopied on fabric, for this sentimental quilt. The photos are of Ruth and Daryl's 1952 wedding and their parents' weddings in 1902 and 1916. The theme blocks were built up as needed with the same fabric later used in the border. Pen-and-ink inscriptions are pieced into adjoining background blocks. Many of the 4"-block fabrics, mostly beiges and grays with a touch of blue, are turned wrong side up for a more muted effect.

JOY AND SORROW ◄

*by Jancy Landry Muensterman,
1991, Santa Rosa, California,
39 ¼" x 39 ¼".*
This quilt was Jancy's entry in
the 1991 Hoffman challenge.
The challenge fabric, a tree
print, is most noticeable in
the plain 4" background squares.
The larger theme block looks
as if it's set on point, an effect
achieved by repeating the light
fabric from the block in the
large Block 1.6 triangles that
adjoin it.

SOMETHING FISHY ◄

*by Marion Eshbach Newell,
1990, Amherst, Massachusetts,
31 ½" x 31 ½".*
In this whimsical quilt, a
tropical fish and a piece of kelp
flow over the theme block's
bright pink frame, joining
company with the dainty
appliquéd fish that dart among
the background blocks.

HARLEY ▶

by Colleen Rowell, 1994, Island Park, New York, 41" x 34". Made in an Alex Dupre class, Colleen's quilt honors her son's Canine Companions for Independence service dog, trained to assist people in wheelchairs. The Labrador-retriever theme block is a silk-screen print, framed with two rounds of narrow strips. Colleen thoughtfully included Flying Geese for the dogs to retrieve.

ALASKA BEARS ▶

by Linda Parkhouse, 1991, Eagle River, Alaska, 17¼" x 21¼". Linda made this quilt for a newborn nephew, using a realistic bear print as the theme: "I didn't want him to be frightened by the bears, so I created a background that had movement and interest of its own. I wanted the bears to appear gradually as he looked at the quilt." (Collection of Sandra J. Marshall)

JORDAN'S QUILT

by Jane M. Buys, 1994, Lynden, Washington, 42" x 58".
Pieced bears from Margaret Rolfe's *Go Wild with Quilts* dominate this pleasant woodland scene, made to celebrate the birth of Jane's nephew, Jordan. The 4" deer blocks and the inner border are airbrushed fabrics by FL-AIR Fabric Design. Note how the "chain" of deer blocks is echoed in the smaller checkerboards just above. (Collection of Jordan S. Douma)

About the Author

Judy Hopkins is a prolific quiltmaker whose fondness for traditional design goes hand in hand with an unwavering commitment to fast, contemporary cutting and piecing techniques. Judy has been making quilts since 1980 and working full-time at the craft since 1985. Her primary interest is in multiple-fabric quilts; most of her pieces are inspired by classic historic quilts in a variety of styles. Her work has appeared in numerous exhibits and publications.

Teaching and writing are by-products of Judy's intense involvement in the process of creating quilts. As a teacher, Judy likes to function as a "structural engineer," providing a basic framework that allows students to focus on creative choices and produce quilts that carry a personal imprint. She is the author of *One-of-a-Kind Quilts, Fit To Be Tied, Around the Block with Judy Hopkins*, and *Down the Rotary Road with Judy Hopkins*, and co-author (with Nancy J. Martin) of *Rotary Riot* and *Rotary Roundup*.

For the last several years, Judy has been working primarily from the scrap bag. Faced with a daunting accumulation of scraps and limited time to deal with them, she started looking for ways to apply quick-cutting methods to scrap fabrics. This led to the design of Judy's popular ScrapMaster ruler, a tool for quick cutting half-square triangles from irregularly shaped scraps,

and the accompanying Blocks and Quilts for the ScrapMaster series. Judy also creates and markets mail-order mystery classes for quilting groups along with mystery patterns for individual quilters, and writes a regular mystery pattern series for *Lady's Circle Patchwork Quilts* magazine.

Judy lives in Anchorage, Alaska, with her husband, Bill, and their Labrador retriever. She has two grown daughters and three adorable and brilliant grandchildren who like to help her sew. Judy is active in her local guild, the Anchorage Log Cabin Quilters, and teaches regularly at the Anchorage quilt shop featured in That Patchwork Place's The New American Quilt Shop Series book, *Calicoes and Quilts Unlimited*.

NOTES

Publications and Products

Many titles are available at your local quilt shop.
For more information, write for a free color catalog
to Martingale & Company, PO Box 118, Bothell,
WA 98041-0118 USA.

☎ U.S. and Canada, call **1-800-426-3126** for the
name and location of the quilt shop nearest you.
Int'l: 1-425-483-3313   **Fax:** 1-425-486-7596
E-mail: info@patchwork.com
Web: www.patchwork.com   1.98